Postcards from Heaven

www.postcardsfromheavenbook.com

Also by Martin Van Horn

When He Speaks:
Deciphered Scripture, Inspired Poetry, and
an Outpouring of Blessings.

www.whenhespeaks.com

POST CARDS from Heaven

Heaven imagined and reported

Martin Van Horn

Life Connections Media
Louisville, Kentucky

Postcards from Heaven Copyright © 2011 by Martin Van Horn. All rights reserved. Printed in the United States of America. No part of this book may be used or reproduced in any manner whatsoever without written permission except in the case of brief quotations embodied in critical articles and reviews. For information, visit www.postcardsfromheavenbook.com or address Life Connections Media, 657 South Hurstbourne Pkwy, Suite 259, Louisville, KY 40222.

Life Connections Media books may be purchased for educational, business, or sales promotional use. For information please write: Life Connections Media, 657 South Hurstbourne Pkwy, Suite 259, Louisville, KY 40222.

To book Martin Van Horn for a speaking engagement, visit www.whenhespeaks.com.

For more information about this book or other materials from Life Connections Media, visit www.lifeconnectionsmedia.com

FIRST EDITION

Designed by Joel Van Horn

Library of Congress Cataloging-in-Publication Data has been applied for.

ISBN-13: 978-0615518015

Acknowledgements

It pays to ask God your questions. I was reading Romans chapter 8 and I asked Him, "What is my inheritance with Christ?" There was no immediate answer, but in the following months I was privileged to dialog with Him further. I asked, "Why is revival singing so loud?" "Because Heaven is loud," He said. Receiving immediate answers to questions makes for exciting Bible study! Each new insight led to another, expanding my sense of the holy rock concert, love feast, garden library and military training camp that is Heaven.

I want to thank some of the people who encouraged me as I turned the Bible's descriptions into my stories and poems. Sharon Van Horn and Mary Thompson, my fellow directors at Life Connections International were always confident my book would be a blessing to many. Joel and Rebekka Van Horn provided invaluable editing, graphics and layout services. Don and Sheila Kimball invested prayer and finances in this publication. Whitney Moore, Pat and Debbie Pazdziora and Mike Hendren gave me vital feedback. Thanks go to countless friends who have prayed. Lynn Breslow, Audrey Longstaff, Gerhard and Maria Schaffer represent people in America, England and Austria. I also want to thank Dr. Brian Simmons of Gateway Christian Fellowship for providing a spiritual atmosphere where my receptivity to God's communication was cultivated.

My privilege has been to share my pictures of our future Home with dear ones preparing to go there. I think of David Longstaff and his friend Keith Jones. I think of my parents, still with us but ready to go any time the Lord comes for them. If I can reflect a spark of Heavenly Father's flaming love waiting for His children then I am grateful.

Foreword

A Foreword by Simon Peter, one of The Twelve and an Apostle, a Sent One, who is enthralled by Jesus Christ:

Written to all of you, who are equally precious to Him, because you trust in the righteous life of our God and Rescuer, Jesus Christ. May you experience more and more of the grace and peace in God and Jesus, our Lord.

Each of us has experienced this Person, who wooed us by His own glory and beautiful character. He decided to entrust to us everything He had in His divine power to make our lives exciting and godly. We have read of His precious commitment to us in His overwhelming promises: in fact He has worked out a way to have us share in His divine nature. We have answered His heart's cry to flee from the fatal corruption destroying the world through our human lusts.

But don't let your experience stop at your decision to trust your life to the Lord; you need to grow into this divine potential. Don't fall back into the enticements of the world. You need to actively apply yourself to expanding your faith. You fell in love with Jesus' wonderful character, His love and compassion, His forthrightness and confidence. Now seek to develop your character to be like His. Of course, you will need knowledge to figure out what you need to do. Since you will find out that Jesus is no theory, you will have to apply disci-

---

* *Taken from St. Peter's second letter, chapter 1, verses 1 to 11, and from chapter 4, verses 13 and 14* pline and self-control to keep learning and developing.

We all find we don't develop as quickly and easily as we would like, so you will need patience and marathon-running endurance. Eventually your human resources will run out, so you will fall into the Lord's arms and receive His grace and power. This will bring you into new depths of prayer and worship. As you worship Him, He will give you His heart for your believing brothers and sisters. You will open yourself to them and learn to love them, but when you get hurt, turn to the Lord, who is the great Lover, and the only source of the divine love that never quits.

I am describing a process, not just a goal. In your growing, you will not dry up or be unproductive. In fact you will experience more of our Lord Jesus Christ, learning to see yourself and other people as He sees. No pain or trouble will touch you, which has not already hurt Him. We dare not become religious, just setting up rules for ourselves, as though we could follow them and be good enough. No, instead we find out how wonderful He is in His love and how much He has to cleanse us from sins. You will find He is doing a mighty work, cleansing you from old feelings, habits, and unholy ways.

Don't stop growing. Remember how He wooed you and grabbed your heart and gave you a new life. Keep that flame alive every day. I don't want you to stumble and fall, no matter how close you are to the final goal. Go for it! Go for it all!

Someday, your growing experience will make you more at Home in the Eternal World than in this one. All of your sacrifices and service and character development will be rewarded. You will be greeted by all those who have been blessed by your life, when you enter the gates of the Eternal Kingdom of our Lord and Rescuer, Jesus Christ. No matter how poor or rich you were down here on earth, in His kingdom you will be welcomed and recognized and richly rewarded by the King Himself.

Rejoice today in the people along the parade route, who will thank you and congratulate you for reflecting Jesus' beautiful divine character and glory.

We are awaiting the new heavens and a new earth with which He promised to replace this one. They will be through *and through right and lovely. Therefore, my beloved brothers and sisters, actively cleanse your lives of any spots and blemishes Jesus points out. That way you will already be at peace with Him when He comes back to earth to do away with the old and bring in His new world.*

Peter was encouraging believers to persevere and grow and look forward to arriving in heaven. I wrote Postcards from Heaven to my son and daughter and to you for the same purposes. I want to thrill to my grand entrance through the Pearly Gates of Jesus' Kingdom. That's why I seek to mature in pleasing my Lord every day. My joy on that day will only be an ounce compared to the Heavenly Father's ton of excitement.

This book represents my invitation along with the call of the Father and Jesus and the Holy Spirit to come join us and celebrate your arrival at our eternal Home.

Prologue

This is it! My end is near. You only know where you put your hope when there is nothing left to hope for.

Lying here looking up at the patchy ceiling of the clinic room, I can think of all the things I want to happen that aren't going to happen. I want to get out and tell people the truth. I want to see you again and hug you and tell you I have always loved you dearly and I always will. I want to be healthy and pain-free again, just like in the days of jogging and sleeping and healthy food. But that will be no more....

I always said, I put my hope in God, in what His Son Jesus did for me. Today it had better be real. No more trying to believe. Either I do or I don't. I prayed so often to change people and circumstances. Now I can't change anything. No health, no money, no freedom are left. What's done is done.

What will happen when I die? Will I be condemned for failures? For missing the goals I wanted to set? Will I be ashamed to see Him and be compared to all the heroes of heaven? Will the King give me thumbs up...or thumbs down?

My conscience plagues me. The great Door to Infinity gets nearer by the hour. The tormentors' voices whisper, "All in vain! Woe to you, weak fool! Lecherous glutton! What makes you think you're going to have it any better now? You lose!" Patients are kept separated, so we can't encourage each other in our end of life desperation.

But I know who my hope is. He has always been there for me. We have walked together all these years, since He came to me with good news. My sin, my crookedness, my shame, my weakness were taken away. How? He took them upon Himself! He won't change when I see Him face to face. That's why I have hope, when there is nothing else to hope for.

I feel weaker. Can't think very well. Should I say I give in? ...Yes, it is finished.

But, look! I can see them! They're coming for me!

Postcards from Heaven

Dear Bekka & Joel

Postcards from Heaven

Heaven Imagined and Reported

by Martin Van Horn

Wow, kids, I can hardly believe I've arrived!

Out of the darkness
Into the light
Leaving the familiar
Bursting into a new world of life

Where am I? Who will I be?
Like a baby being born
I'm an adult reborn into a world of light

Eyes astonished
Mouth agape
Better than I could have imagined

This is reality
Heaven is our Home

The last few minutes were terrible! I was weak and disoriented. As I lost strength, I got weaker and drowsy, flickering into awareness. Soon the pain drifted from my consciousness and everything around me seemed far away. As I closed my eyes, I was not sure what I was seeing. I said I was ready to go, and then Someone else took over. I just went along for the ride. Light came at me, from in front or above, I can't say. Two angels were suddenly on either side of me. Their sense of authority and peace rolled over me like a breaking wave. I was in good hands, supremely sturdy hands.

You know the descriptions: young, manly, dressed in blazing white with gold bands across their chests, a sword at their waists. It was a shock to see and touch them: they were real! It turns out the invisible world is affecting us all the time, but we don't sense it. In my situation, the angels weren't the only invisible characters coming after me.

The Dark Angels had assigned some demons to try one last time to grab me and drag me down to darkness with them. They are so damnably persistent, even though they know I belong to the One who bought me and keeps me. I could look down and see the gray-green, shadowy hounds of darkness snarling at my feet, trying to hold me with their claws and intimidate me with their fangs and cold breath. They are ugly gargoyles, dark, cold, smelly and nasty. As though I were like all the mortals being dragged into the maw of their Prince with the heart of ice, who rules darkness with an iron fist. Saying all those old things about me, they tried one more time to paint me as black as they are. I would indeed have been a "lecherous glutton, a wavering coward, a puny failure," if I had not been cleansed. By myself I probably would have fainted into their wide-open fangs.

Praise God, they are no match for holy angels. There was no wild fistfight; only the authoritative, "Be gone, you servants of Satan!" And it was over. The two angels had their swords drawn, but were just as serene as if the demons were not there at all. All in an eternity's work for them, I guess. Grace and Mercy introduced themselves as my Companions. They said it was their privilege to escort the Father's child to His Home. I guess we flew; at least we covered a long distance in a short amount of time. Always more light, brighter and brighter blue-white light gave the only direction.

Instead of staring up at the ceiling, I was looking down at my body and wondering who that was down there on the cot. In the permeating white light: earth and you, my loved ones, were far away. I even forgot I was leaving everyone behind. That time seems so long ago, so much has happened.

I have no idea how long it has been for you since I left you behind. I decided to send you a few postcards describing what the human heart longs for: this place called "Home." Because it has always been God's Home and He is a big God: it is a vast place, busy with fascinating scenery, people, Beings, music, perfumes and activities. Earth was always intriguing, but Home goes beyond human imagining, so please be patient.

It's all I've ever dreamed! And it's so much more besides! No wonder the others, who wrote before me, said that their words couldn't describe this place. So how strange that I am trying to tell you what it is like up here. Now that I've settled in, I know this is where I've always wanted to be. People everywhere below have longed to be in this place, but never were quite sure it was real. Well, it is real, more real than anything on earth. There is such harmony among all the people and Beings and the plants and animals, that we are all glad it will always be this way.

Always is the key word. I've experienced so much already; it would take a lifetime to describe. But that's your lifetime I'm talking about. I have the time. Mine will be a life of unending, joyful surprises. It's a good thing I left my old body behind. It was getting pretty tired, and I'm sure it couldn't stand the pace.

First, the light: everywhere I'm penetrated by light. For centuries visionaries have exclaimed over the loving, peaceful white light of glory. That is what visitors experience who have to go back to earth. Paradise is a garden where everything shines so brightly that the air and the mountains all look white to earthlings. But there is more. The Lord of Glory has a throne from which He rules the universe. He shines like brilliant blue lightning. The throne is surrounded by a rainbow of light that looks like the sparkling green of an emerald.

Ever see a healthy plant with not just shiny leaves, but also a bright light inside? Of course not! Well, here the trees shine because they too are penetrated by light: polished bronze, brass, gold. They are not dark trunks, green leaves, and bright blossoms. Instead the golden leaves reflect the emerald rainbow of the Throne itself. It's the opposite of Earth's yellow sun and green leaves, but you get some of the same effect. Imagine vines yielding precious jewels for blossoms!

The rocks sparkle green, blue, yellow, white, and on and on. And they don't reflect sunshine; they each glow like a light bulb. On earth, if the sun went dark, there would be no light. At Home you don't see any sun, because everything shines. Back then I would have had to put on sunglasses to stand this glare, but here I have new eyeballs, built for this radiance. My skin would have scorched but now I have a new body that glows with spirit, like God's own flaming tongues of fire.

Are the rocks and trees and grass hot from glowing? I can't tell any more. If you touch the photograph of hot, glowing red charcoal, is the photo hot? No, but you know the coals are supposed to be burning hot. That's what this place looks like. It's just that I must be as hot as every object around me.

And then there's the sound, the music in the air. My ears must be new as well, because how could you stand a 24-hour concert at blowout volume? Lightning bolts flashing into the sky power this concert for more than a million ticket holders. When the Source of All Power thunders His love and the lightning bolts dazzle our hearts, the waterfall voices vibrate our bodies with song that fits our joy perfectly. The Spirit keeps us pumped up without ever wearing us out. Back at Madison Square Garden I wore earplugs to make that music livable. Joel, you said your ears were ringing afterward. In your friend's truck, his subwoofer boomed but crushed my lungs so I couldn't breathe. Think how much our new bodies have to endure in the concert of glory. Worship streams from the beautiful Composer into our hearts and back out again through our lips. Together our voices chorus the breadth of our effortless joy to the musical throne.

We all can hear and sing along all the time. And the Leader's voice! Sweet and overwhelming at the same time, we all stop to listen and sing along. Then every so often a whole group arrives. Their Enemy on Earth released them to come Home and they get together to sing a New Song. I never get tired of being caught up by the Song Leader and his choirs. I can hardly wait to go join them after I finish writing this postcard. Bekka, your lovely voice has always been a blessing to me, so up here even more people will get blessed.

The air: even breathing is a special occasion. Summer residents used to come to the ocean shore to breathe the salt air. Hikers trekked steep mountainsides to inhale pine forest freshness. Well our air is alive! Remember the aroma of lemon squeezed, or oranges being peeled, or a bottle of cinnamon just opened? Remember the surprise of soda bubbles up your nose? Boing! They wake you up. They refresh your head. Imagine, every breath you breathe is this exhilarating. That's why I love being here and standing around enjoying air. Not only are the flowers and trees fragrant, but every time angel wings fly by, they leave new perfume behind. But I can tell every time the Lord walks in His garden, because the scent always turns my head to say, "Wow, what was that aroma? It's so refreshing!"

The inhabitants: What made our house such a special place was you living in it, together with mom and me. We tried to decorate the rooms to express who we were and to make guests feel welcome in our home. It was where we wanted to be and hoped others would enjoy as well. Our eternal Home is not just a place either; it's Father as host and it's people that make me feel settled and relaxed. Beside the people, the Beings treat us with love and respect. We have no strangers here. You know who the others are as soon as you meet, and meeting is always fun, not scary. Before you meet you are sure they love you! Not at all like Earth, except for the good parts.

On planet Earth they would have been foreign: hairstyle, skin color, body build, unintelligible language. I'd be asking myself: "Are they dangerous? Do I like them? How powerful are they? How educated? Skillful? Approachable?" Now I can talk to anyone, no problem, no language barrier. They say one of the features of heaven is the honesty. Our Host knows everything and we know everything about everybody. We've all gotten over the shock of meeting Him when we got here. Secrets all came out into the open and were dealt with. It was a shocker. What a relief it has been, being healed and renewed and relaxed!

Let me fill you in on what happened to me since I left you and my mortal friends behind. People used to call my leaving "my birthday," but now we just call it death. They used to rejoice, because we are following our Lord, who died but rose up from the grave and went to heaven to prepare the way for the rest of us. So departing earth actually means "birthday" in heaven. We used to celebrate you kids, bringing together friends, food, decorations, fun and presents. Well, that's the celebration that surprised me here.

I've only given you hints of the life here. I have to bring you into contact with the Host, whose Home this is. We humans are invited children, formed by Him to share His love and His work. We can only enter in if we have been prepared. Wanting to come or trying to be good enough for the guest list don't cut it. You see the Host is a living fire. The reason everything here glows is because His fire shines in everything He has made for Himself.

We are like moths. The flame stands out in the dark and we want it, so we fly toward the warmth. Inside me the longing for reality said, "Aha!" to the lure of delight beyond any passing itch. Then we find out when we arrive it burns, because it is hot enough to consume everything that is not already on fire. Once entranced by the Living One, we can't go back; we must meet Him. "Here I come! "

In my heart I knew the One who created me also loved me. He showed me that by how much He was willing to sacrifice to have me: not a thing, but instead His dear child, His son. Since He said Jesus' sacrifice of his blood dying on the cross was enough, I trusted it was enough for me. The Host invited me and cleansed me, so I knew I would get through the door. But just as my mortal body could not stand up to the light, heat, sound or joy in this place; I knew my spirit was not adequate to endure the outpouring holy fire of the actual presence of God.

I must tell you how He made me adequate, not just for this place but also for His presence.

Dear Bekka & Joel

Postcards from Heaven

Heaven Imagined and Reported

by Martin Van Horn

I'm so glad my insecurities were unjustified. Now I can relax.

Fear and Trembling

Living in godly fear of the One who Judges all men at His Throne

Ahead, seeing the gate of pearl
The walls of diamond
The streets of gold

What will I have to hear?
"Surprise Party!"

Dear Bekka and Joel,

Somehow I knew when we three had arrived. The white light began to reveal visible features: gleaming floor or street, gilded white columns brighter than marble, a piazza filled with people clothed in shimmering white robes. I also knew the One there to meet me.

I could not take my eyes off Him. Not His clothes or glowing feet and hair transfixed me; it was His smiling eyes. It's a good thing He smiled, because the blazing fire in His eyes almost knocked me over. "Jesus!" was all I said. Like his friend John visiting heaven, I wanted to fall on my face. I wanted to pour out thanks for loving me, cleaning me, rescuing me from the Dark Angels and their prince, bringing me to his Home, being there for me. All these feelings exploded in me at once. Out of my mouth came only, "I love you."

I fell down on my knees in awe and gratitude. I was filled with wonder at His glory and beauty. I wanted to spend the rest of my days with Him. Then I fell down on my face, overwhelmed, if not crushed, with the privilege of being here and seeing Him as He really is. Seeing Him meant seeing me, a poor creation out of dust, now a friend of the Almighty Friend, the Ruler of the universe.

Then His voice washed over me, "Get up, Martin." He reached down to lift me. His touch and His voice made me sparkle inside. I laughed, I cried, I leaped up and spun around, arms in the air. Only as I was spinning did I start to notice my surroundings.

My Lord Jesus was in front of me and I had the impression we were in a vast open colonnade with a wide avenue leading into the distance. My Host's face glowed golden brown with shiny white hair, as though He were infinitely old, yet youthfully vigorous. Everyone I had ever met on earth wanted something from me—approval, love, help, words or whatever. Now in front of me stood One who wanted and needed nothing from me, but only poured out eagerness and understanding. He loves me because He wants to, and He acts as though He really likes me. Because He's glad I'm here, I am too. I just love Him back; I want to be with Him.

He gestured to come with Him down the avenue. As we walked, I stared at him. Jesus glows with life, and everything around us shines, but we were heading toward a more glorious light. I can only compare it to standing in a sunlit forest, walking toward the sunrise coloring the sky with more and more color, brighter and brighter. As we walked I found out my first impression was false. We were not surrounded by mere stone columns, but by rows of people of all races and expressions, all different heights and features. Yet the bigger surprise was how glad they were to see me.

We couldn't be strangers, even though some of us were meeting for the first time. My grandmothers came running, my grandfathers, my great-grandparents too. They did not look old, or frail, or old-fashioned. They looked as they must have appeared in their twenties or thirties. As we hugged I heard, "We knew you'd come. We've been praying for you and the family a long, long time." I want to hear their life stories. Yet while they are special as family, it's as though our family had boomed a million times.

Antoine and Piquet thanked me for sending money so they could have food in Haiti. Zhang thanked me for praying for China, so he could preach the Gospel. Karl gripped me and thanked me for handing him that tract in the market square in Austria. If you can believe it, I remember everyone's name as I never could before; they're all my friends. Immediately I know who each one is and what they mean to me. I don't have space to write about all of them. We have time to share our "glory stories." But now my parade was headed for the Throne.

Even with Jesus leading me by the hand, I found my footsteps getting heavier, my skin warming, my eyes burning, my knees weakening. Surrounded by this incomprehensible love and overwhelming light, I felt completely out of place. I was nobody, surrounded by somebodies. I was weak, but they were confident. My impurity became completely obvious, with nothing to hide me. God is a fire, jealous and pure. He burns up all that is not like Him. I was starting to fear.

Jesus roared to an angel ahead. We now had not only thousands or more people around us, but also more and more angels. Some were eight feet high; some were fifteen feet high. All were robed in short white robes, belted with gold. Some were awesomely impressive. "Kabodaiah! Bring the hot coal!" One of the big, impressive angels went closer to the Throne, where an altar flamed not only up, but in all directions. He took fire tongs and removed a glowing coal. Then I saw him coming toward me. Yikes!

Pure fire meeting plain flesh: what could happen except to burn me up? Words cannot describe what He did. On earth you want things. You try to make life go your way. You want to be happy, even if not everybody is happy with you. Right? That's the way I was. I wanted you to love me and listen adoringly to me. I wanted to have money to buy whatever I desired, and give you gifts to make you happy. I used to pray to God to do my will. I searched the Bible to make me a wise person, so I could convince people of the way I believed. I wanted people to know how great I was, but not trap me or show up my weaknesses. Sound familiar? Basically, I wanted to be the center of my own kingdom.

But now I was in the presence of The King, the King of the Universe, the king over all kings everywhere and always. No place remained for "King Me." The burning fire of God was about to remove the "Me." The coal was itself fire, blue, green, white, yellow. It contacted my lips and my whole body burst into flame. Like looking over the edge of the Grand Canyon, I felt dizzy and about to fall into a bottomless emptiness. I lost. I lost what I thought I had to have. Burned up were my desire, my grasping, my reputation, my accomplishments, my substitute things that could not satisfy. Shriveled to nothingness were awards, possessions, titles, resentful thoughts and grandiose plans. King Me had lived in perpetual frustration, and now he was gone. The sound of "FOOMP!" sums it up best.

The coal of fire consumed me. I am not the same person, but I am still myself. Instead of fingers grasping to hold on, I live with a child's open hand to let Him plunk into my life all the good gifts He has treasured in His heart since Forever. God's Word describes things God hates and forbids. I had grown to agree with Him, but I could not always shake loose from my life these plagues neither of us wanted. They seemed glued to me even though I pled with the Holy Spirit to purify me. My

Father saw my heart and heard my groans. Now my begging is over. All I down deep desired, all I longed for, all of God Himself came pouring into my new self. How can I describe blessed peace, piercing joy and arousing anticipation all at the same time?

Now I knew I could stand the Glory Fire of the One on the Throne.

Odd as it seems, the more tears shed on earth, the fewer get shed here. I am so taken back by how narrow, how selfish, how unbelieving I have been. I could weep over the goodness of God shown to miserable King Me. He wanted me, created me, redeemed me, and taught me about real life. All that so I could be ungrateful? accusing Him of not listening, not caring? Many times I wept down there. I could weep again, but Jesus is here, right by my side. "Do not weep, Martin. I have seen your tears. Now you shall be comforted." And it was as though all my sadness were wiped away when He wiped away my tears!

"Martin, I put a new heart in you. It's a heart like mine. You struggled to express it, but I was with you through it all. Now your body is acceptable to my Father and your heart is pure, so you get to see Him. This is what eternal life is all about!"

Dear Bekka & Joel

Postcards from Heaven

Heaven Imagined and Reported

by Martin Van Horn

It used to be a struggle to be good.
Now I see how it is worth it.

It's war: Me vs. Me!
Will I ever be pure?

Jacob wrestled with God's angel
But sister Corrie said
"Don't wrestle, just nestle"

Our Father, who art in Heaven
Holy is Your Name

At last! Holiness pays!

Dear Bekka and Joel,

You know how people say, "When I get to heaven, I'm going to ask God why this thing happened?" I had plenty of questions myself.

But at this point we were approaching the center of the universe, the King of Time and Eternity, the Judge of all creatures. Saints of all ages have longed for a glimpse of what holy angels gaze at every day forever. They are never bored, their wings are covered with eyes inside and outside so they continually find more aspects of Sovereign God to praise and worship. (You see, even angels are finite, but God is unlimited and always new.) The Seraphim burn in His presence with divine, unrelenting glory. With two wings they cover their faces, with two they cover their feet, and with two they fly, suspended around the Throne. Their worship shakes the whole mountaintop with "Holy! Holy! Holy! Awesome beauty of our God!". Now here was little old Martin, right in the middle.

Jesus confidently held my hand and boomed out, "Father, I am so happy to introduce my brother, Martin Van Horn! You chose him for me ages ago. You gave him to me on my cross. I have been faithful to keep him and bring him Home. He has confessed my Name before men and now I confess him to You as my own."

Jesus looked me in the eyes and said, "Welcome to my Home. It's your Home too." In His hand appeared a white stone. On my stone was my new name. You'll have to come join me to hear more about it. You'll get one for yourself some day.

Then Father spoke. No one on earth could have stood up to His voice. Compare it to Niagara Falls speaking human words. The Holy Spirit is the fountainhead of the River of Life. He poured out through Father's pronouncement, "Bring Martin's new clothes."

I step into the River of Life, the cleansing, healing stream. Another angel brought white garments. I don't know how, but suddenly I was wearing them. They fit perfectly. Even the white fabric, or whatever it is, glows. I actually looked down for the first time to look at myself. I could see the clothes, but I could see me too. The robe represents who I am, instead of covering up who I am. People can even hear my robes telling them my story, my activities that pleased God. My body is so alive! My skin glows too. My eyes can take the light. My ears can take the roar of the crowds. And roar they did. This time it was for me!

I never wanted to be a movie star (good thing, right?). Now I was the star of heaven's crowd. The people and the angels shouted together, "Praise to our God and to the Lamb. They chose Martin and made him worthy to live forever. The plan of God is coming to completion. The Bride of Christ is making herself ready. Glory to the Lamb, who is our Bridegroom!" Suddenly we were all singing together, and I knew the words. It was the same as when I communicate up here, I know what they mean and they know what I wanted to say. We all joined in the song of the Lamb:

Great and marvelous are your works,
Lord God Almighty; just and true are your ways,
O King of saints.

Incredibly delicious has everything been this far. But more happened to blow my mind, even though it has all been promised to the saints for thousands of years, earth time. Jesus started walking forward, toward the Throne. The One who sits there is all energy, pouring out light, lightnings, speaking thunders, shining as a rainbow. Looking up I saw wings and faces all around us. The four living Creatures tower 90 feet over the Throne. Each has four faces: a gentle ox, a regal lion, a sharp-eyed eagle, a glorious man. Their wings reached out to one another over the Glory. Their glowing gold bodies build a wall of strength.

I glanced down and saw an ocean, clear as glass, except that reddish gold flames flared through sections of it. Instead of clear liquid mixed with pink liquid, it was as though someone occasionally added liquid fire and then stirred. Each section only blazed for a second until another area lit up in its place. Everywhere was movement, not foam or seaweed or fish, but waves lapping and divine fire leaping.

Now I know what happened that night back on earth, while the 12 disciples battled the wind and rain in their fishing boat on the Sea of Galilee. Jesus had remained back on land that night. The men were afraid for their lives on the stormy lake, while he spent the night up here on heaven's water with his father (we call it "prayer"). When it was time to rejoin the men, Jesus just kept walking on the water, like he was still back Home, except now it was the water the twelve followers were sailing on. Of course, the men in the boat freaked out when they saw him strolling across the waves. (Only Peter wanted to try walking on the earthly water where he sailed his fishing boat.) Here we all walk on water, on the crystal sea of Home.

Our Father's throne is like the snowy, blinding peak of His holy mountain. Just as we see clouds driven by the wind and storms on the summits, so He boils with life, rumbles with thunders of love and judgment, pours out clouds of glory and being, and the waterfall of Spirit sprays. The geyser never stops. It sounds like a waterfall and flows out and away as a crystal ocean. Always flowing, always moving, but holding millions, billions of worshippers on its glassy wavelets.

I could tell Jesus felt entirely at Home here as he led me to the seat of His Father, our Father. Where the energy and thunders had been off-putting, actually standing on the Throne was reassuringly calm and homey. The center of the universe is also the fatherly lap of my Creator and my best friend. As far as I was concerned the galaxies stopped spinning and the angels' music was all for me. This is the One to whom I have given my life, my faith, my prayers, my sacrifices, my money, my efforts and now He is glad to see me. He knows me and I know why I love Him. He has done everything all for me: a planet, a sun, weather, birth, health, you and Sharon, family and friends, fellow saints, work to accomplish, problems to solve, books to write, and on and on. Bless Him, bless Him forever! My joy is flowing and increasing; and somehow His joy is over-flowing too.

Wait till I tell you about what He gave me that He couldn't share until I got here.

Dear Bekka & Joel

Postcards from Heaven

Heaven Imagined and Reported

by Martin Van Horn

Jesus' Sermon on the Mount seemed so unrealistic. Now I see what He was talking about.

Blessed are the Kingdom dwellers
On earth
For they have tasted
And "It is good!"

Come Kingdom of God!
Come on earth!
We can hardly wait

Dear Bekka and Joel,

Jesus told us about "our Father in heaven" from his personal experience. On earth I could only begin to creep up on an approximation of what he meant. Now I have sat on the lap of my heavenly Father. I have sat with Him on His throne. You can do it from down on earth today; today you can enter within the Veil that sets apart the Holy of Holies, where He lives. Take advantage of the intimacy He offers so you will enjoy Him when you get here too.

Have you ever wondered how our Heavenly Father can attend to the prayers of billions of people, all at the same time? I still don't know how it works, but while I was sitting with Him, there was no rush; I had the Father's cheerful attention all to myself, but if I told you everything we talked about, it would probably take weeks. Earth time is a narrow thread of disappearing moments. Here it is a broad plain of rest. There is no push; there is always time to do God's will. From one moment to the next can be a thousand years, if needed.

> Father confided, "Now you may enter into the eight blessings of heaven that my Son, the King, explained about. He described his kingdom in that sermon on a mountain in Israel.
>
> "Because you recognized the emptiness of everything temporary, everything visible, you knew you were poor. I love it when you recognize yourself to be empty-handed, but open hearted, so I can bestow the riches I have always intended for you. Now you will receive my promised glory, knowledge, purity and unspeakable joy at my hand. I have given you family and wealth and your own domain to rule forever. That's why the poor are blessed: I give them my Kingdom to rule with me."

Instantly a flame ignited in my heart, in my head, in my belly. This Father's desire to give his children the Kingdom was such an overwhelming gift. I felt gratitude, humility, wonder, and excitement. My human heart had always been too small. How could God love so many people? It was too much for my narrow, hard heart. But now I burned with a new love, the Father's love. A brand new, eternal body to enjoy my Home came with a fresh fire inside to share my Father's enthusiasm and pain.

"Second, while you were on earth you were all torn up about your shortcomings and excesses, your sin, the evil in your heart. You mourned for what sin had done in your life, your family, your society and in the world. You cried out to me for my will to be done on earth and rule there as I rule in heaven. My son took your pain as his own suffering. I comforted him with my peace and my joy. Now you too will be comforted by the joy in my heart. Everything you endured in the kingdom of the Deceiver will disappear into faint, momentary nothingness. Instead you will feel the overwhelming weight of my glory. But I have made you strong. Your new, eternal body is a spiritual body. You are no longer weak in your flesh. My heart of confidence will give you delight in my every word instead of doubting and you will please me in every work. We will live and work and feast together forever and ever."

I was shocked again. He means there is more; there's always more.

"On earth you submitted to me in faith. My Spirit was strong in your weakness and He made you trustworthy so I could give you work in my kingdom. The third blessing is happiness I only give to the meek. Just as I gave the land of Israel on loan to the nation of Abraham to cultivate, utilize and defend, so also I have much to give you as well. Each tribe and family received an allotment in the land. This was their inheritance forever, but it belonged to me and I watched over it closely. The earthly land was a down payment on this heavenly property. You get an inheritance too.

"All believers in Jesus my King will receive an eternal allotment in our heavenly land, but this time it will not be on loan. On earth you were a faithful administrator to the One who lent you temporary things like air, food, land, possessions, work, health, family and friends, etc. Now you get to keep the things that are truly yours. I know what will delight your heart, because I made you and know you through and through. I saw the flowers you planted and the weeds you pulled and the water you sprinkled, just to celebrate a bed of daffodils and marigolds for a few days. You tried to preserve some beauty by taking photos. I know some projects that will challenge you and fulfill you for a long, long time. Relax and enjoy! No one will steal it, or make fun of it, or pressure you. It's yours. When you see your domain, you will see how you have been giving my Son His building materials.

"Your every act of trust, your every obedience was like a jewel, a pillar of gold, a table of silver, a tile of marble to be used in your eternal house. Those times you forgave your betrayers are now pearls of great price, made from your suffering. Because you let me be your avenger, instead of taking things into your own hands, those surrenders are now brilliant crystal. Harsh circumstances brought you to the point of agreeing with me about your neediness. Your willingness to be vulnerable has created for you a garden of strong trees and delicate vines. And because you still worshipped me and sang songs of faith in your pain, you have created windows to let my glory into your permanent Home. Your glimpses of my joy have now become my blossoms of ecstasy. "

I wanted to cry, not from pain, but from seeing Father's sensitivity, the way He knows how I feel and wants me to have real satisfaction. Suffering and faith let Him into my life to do something good for something bad. Gratefulness for blessings let Him be God, where I could have invented idols. Now He wants me to have what I want and I enjoy. He can trust my new heart, my heavenly desires, my yielding to Him in all things.

"Once you knew things were not the way they should be. You got mad. You tried to change people and circumstances. But then you saw all humans are faulty and society is oppressive, stuck in the claws of the Oppressor. You cried out to me for divine, heavenly righteousness, such as you seldom see on earth. Desperate for a better nature in yourself, and better relationships around you, you put your hope in what only I could accomplish, even if I chose to use you to work with me. In heaven your dreams are going to be fulfilled. The fourth happiness of heaven is to see everything being right, happy, flowing and growing. My Spirit pervades everything. All things rejoice to be the way they are and enjoy being together. Everything fits harmoniously and grows. This includes you; you fit in, and everyone likes you. The little parade on the way to my throne gave you a taste of your welcome."

On earth I had a few friends and the times we had together took us to low points, but also to heights of sharing that made it so worthwhile. We cried, but we also laughed. Here I am surrounded by a billion friends without any more tears.

"Formerly strength, speed and deception seemed to rule. People even used generosity like a tool. You thought, 'Good people seem to deserve good things, but bad people definitely deserve bad things to happen to them.' However, you were willing to see all people as needing love and goodness, no matter how they might look. You recognized that even people who do bad things need mercy, not simply justice. You were willing to show mercy to dangerous people, miserable people, people who could not repay you. Now your Father in heaven will repay you out of my merciful heart that you were expressing. You have experienced for yourself why the throne of God is called "The Mercy Seat." The fifth blessing is to meet the One who cares. I have known you forever and my Son delights over you as a gift from me. The Spirit fires you up and makes you the person you were created to be. You now know what it is to be loved! Judgment has been passed and I give you mercy unending.

"Despite all pleasures and possibilities of earth, you decided to seek God beyond everything else. You rejected whatever distracted and sidetracked you from my Beautiful One. I, Jehovah, was your delight and now you get to see me face to face. Your happiness is to have more of the Person you sought after, but could not see. I am the center of heaven. My Home is your Home. What I like, you like too. I look out for your best and delight you and I see your joy. Nothing will ever come between you and me. Your name will never be removed from the Lamb's Book of Life.

"Back on earth you risked your own status and security so other people could experience peace instead of war, chaos, enmity, and destruction. You believed I do not take sides, but that I could introduce a better way, so all could live together peaceably. The next happiness is your reward—security, prosperity, peace. Paradise was once lost, but it has now been restored. Enjoy my pleasure garden! Let's feast together, one eternal family!

"The remaining happiness was counted strange by most; it is

for those who risked reputation, possessions and health to stand by Jesus among his enemies. You suffered pain and loss, you suffered voluntarily as my Son did, to benefit other people by his offer of a better life. Now you will join in a fellowship of war veterans. You kept heaven's perspective on earth's torments. You believed what I said about you, rather than what people said. I consider you worthy to work equally with Abel, Abraham, Moses, Daniel, Hosea, Agabus, my pioneer prophets of the past.

"The King promised to reward faithful servants. You can enter into the King's reward. Jesus did it all to see many brothers and sisters live with him together in his heavenly Home. You helped him accomplish his goal, so you get to share his joy. You will see the people you brought to faith in Jesus through your words and deeds. They will thank you and rejoice with you. Party on!

"Life on earth is short. Happiness does not last and it is tainted with regrets. Heaven is forever. Here everyone is happy permanently. Whenever anyone joins us, our happiness becomes even greater. You will receive more than you ever desired and by receiving you will also be giving. Everything you have is a gift, and here we all are givers. That's why everyone here is so happy! You will never be poor again."

Father, O Father! What can I say? Strength, wisdom, caring are a real father's attractions and He showed them to me. I can rest in His love. He won't change. There are no shadows in His light. I could feel a song bursting from my mouth because my heart was too full to keep it inside.

I've seen beyond the glory.
I've seen beyond the light.
I've seen your heart of love to me
And I'll sing of my delight.

The more I see, the more I want to see:
Your beauty once glimpsed, now a blaze;
Your truth, Your goodness, Your mercy
Calling forth thunderous praise.

Thank You I can see with wondering eyes:
Treasures of Your Father's heart displaying,
Sweet fruit of Your dark sacrifice,
Blessed saints, our crowns before You laying.

Father and Son in eternal communion
Have swept me by Spirit this oneness to join.
O Jesus, you saw me in Father's sweet vision
And went forth to make me Your man.

O Father, what power in humble apparel:
Defeating the Evil by trusting Your will.
He crushed Satan's head and he saved us from hell.
You are our Home: forever together we'll dwell.

I know it's hard to imagine being here and seeing Father in all His glory, but in your spirit you can hear Father calling you and all His children to come Home. I'm sure you've had moments in worship, where you know in your spirit that God is pleased and you sense a connection. It's unseen but it's real. You know it and can't shake the longing, even if the world distracts you a thousand times a day. Your unscratchable itch means Father wants you to be with Him, clean and pure and joyful forever. Until all His children respond, He is not satisfied.

Every day on earth is a gateway to experience Eternity in everyday living. Every time you say, "Yes" to His Spirit calling, you open yourself to let in divine creativity. I can almost see Father rubbing his hands in anticipation of you and Him creating something new together. Maybe you don't know what's going to happen but He has worked on it forever, crafting a unique opportunity for you and Himself, His angel servants and His Spirit of adventure to work together. That's how we fashion a community that shines like a golden network, a city set on a hill. It looks to me from here like one of those legendary "mithril" chain-link shirts in Lord of the Rings.

I got to look down from Father's throne on the River of Time. For each person on earth, time seems like a narrow gutter trickling from birth to death. But it's not. Time is wide, flowing over billions of creatures. Like a gold prospector yearning for yellow glints in a sandy river bed, Father brings together people of faith, who are open to His will. To Him their faith reflects back His own golden beauty. Just as a prospector reaches into the flow of water to gather treasure he will keep, so Father sends forth His Word and Jesus delegates His flaming servants to join believers in this formation of faith and obedience.

For example, I saw a man looking at numbers on apartment doors going down a corridor until an angel prompted him to knock on one. The woman inside slowly stood from her unmade bed, glanced in the mirror, then opened the door. Her gloom immediately brightened as she exclaimed, "God must have sent you!" From up here I saw a spark, a flash. Two believers and their two angels all revealed a glimpse of glory. Two lives had come together, weaving two threads into the everlasting tapestry of love, to be displayed for the family in God's home. As the river flowed on, they continued in conversation, but that golden treasure was still there in the riverbed. Lots of sand and gravel and nasty mud just washed away. Everywhere I looked, there were golden links weaving together over the whole earth, here dense and there thinly spread. Father works it out that the gold lasts, but the mud quickly disappears.

As the Word says, there is a time for everything under heaven. If we synchronize our lives with the good works Father prepares ahead of time, we create golden moments in the flow of "ordinary" life. From His Throne all those golden moments spread out in a beautiful shining pattern of love, blanketing the world.

Dear Bekka & Joel

Postcards from Heaven

Heaven Imagined and Reported

by Martin Van Horn

What a privilege to meet heroes who went before me or I knew on Earth.

Absurd omnipotence

The Lord of Glory
Commander of Armies
Chooses the weak ones of the earth
To be more than conquerors
Over entrenched, mighty Evil

Ha, ha, ha, ha!

Dear Joel and Bekka,

What does God care about?

Turns out, He is not impressed with numbers, size, reputation or riches. He sees everything. What He is doing lasts forever. His will pleases Him and people doing His will are honored here at Home. Some have received much more honor than I have. When you get here you can meet them. While you're still away from Home, you can please Father, and you could even receive honor like these have received. But you have to live by heavenly values down there before you arrive up here.

People up here are honored, who in their former lives were trodden down and overlooked. You would be astounded at the African orphans arrayed in gold, leading the dance circles. And then there are Chinese widows organizing angel battalions. North Korean evangelists hold seminars for scholars and pastors.

Unique is the guerilla fighter executed on the cross next to the Lord on Golgotha. That amazing guy saw past the blood and spit and dirt and cursing. He saw the Jewish King he had been fighting for all his life. He thought he had to kill pagan Roman soldiers to gain Jewish freedom. But that was not how he won the Kingdom for himself. Father must have revealed His son to this accused thief and murderer at the last minute, so he could know his struggle had not been in vain. He even argued with his fellow thief who cursed, saying, "We deserve to die. But this man in the middle has done nothing wrong." To the Lord he asked, "Jesus, remember me when you come into your kingdom." Jesus dying, managed to groan out, "Today you will be with me in Paradise," brought him up here to Paradise first, even though he had done nothing at all. He has a special place of honor because of his supreme faith at the moment of death.

Some of the little things I did were noticed up here more than even I thought about them. God never forgets good things. They even get recorded so others can read about us. It wasn't the Sunday church meetings I so carefully prepared that attracted notice. They were all about the Spirit in God's people anyway. My praying beforehand, the Word of God working in my own heart, the way I let God lead in the meeting: these were noticed. Or the visit to Piroshka in the hospital, the phone call to Sister Jasmine, the music I gave Mary, these things made Father glad. Or the times I asked forgiveness and when I let offenses go. Jesus got the victory. Forgiving is big to God. That makes His heart glad, to see me acting as He desires to act. It set Him free to break off my demons of revenge and self-pity.

Some people could not be released from their sin and condemnation, because they would not let people's offenses go. Jesus warned that God could not give them what they need, because they would not forgive. Some believers were not admitted to their Home, because they would not pass on the freedom Jesus earned for them by his Crucifixion and Victory. Some issues Father is really strict about. We were warned!

Oh joy! My old friend, Elly, from Austria just came through the gate and I got to see her parade. They call her a "war veteran," because she fought the good fight of faith despite overwhelming odds. She was raped and abused at an early age, became a single mom, got married, was dumped for another woman, lost her 3 boys, became ill, lost her job, went on welfare, got retrained, etc., etc. Most of all, she hung in there, receiving good counsel, trusting the Lord in the midst of her trials. What made me glow with joy to see her was the fact that I had a part in encouraging her when she was a baby Christian. She hugged me and told me that what I shared had stuck with her and helped her when she wanted to give up.

That's what I mean. Be like Elly. She suffered and forgave the unjust treatment. God's Spirit was able to speak to her about things she was doing to other people. In her honesty, she did not hide her faults, but let God make her pure and holy. He also sent some of our brothers and sisters to walk with her through her torments.

From the throne everything begins to make sense. Father is the center and source of all good. He wants to give. On earth we did not always see this because we saw other factors that get in His way. After father Adam brought corruption, everything started to decay. Earth became tainted with death through earthquake, storm, disease, drought and fruitlessness. People sought selfish advantage and God's creations became empty mechanisms. Instead of blaming our Enemy, people blamed the

One who loves us. We always try to use Him for our own devices. What a travesty!

Nevertheless, Father was patient. He and the Son had a plan. I now know it was the only plan that could restore His original purpose in making earth and us humans. Jesus not only carried out his mission of reconciliation, but he is now the center of Father's plan for the renewed universe. He cared enough to show me my life. He showed me how I was part of the whole plan of ages past, and of ages to come. The divine Spirit can download in an instant so much that it will take an eternity to understand and appreciate, but that's OK.

On earth everyone puzzles over evil and God's character or power. From here it looks different. Father revealed so much in His Word, but people don't want to see it. Let me give you a general impression of what He said. He has not changed His mind, so it still applies. You have questions about, "Why?" as much as anyone has. Whatever solution you come up with will determine how you look at God and how you live. It is so easy to come up with some human concept that blames our loving Father and our King. Please pay attention to me, even though I seem long-winded.

Dear Bekka & Joel

Postcards from Heaven

Heaven Imagined and Reported

by Martin Van Horn

We used to say, "It's a problem of communication." Now I know why.

Bricks

You throw
And I add to my wall
I throw
And I cannot reach you anymore

Love

He infiltrated my heart
He warms me out of my fortress

Dear Bekka and Joel,

Philosophy and religion have complicated so much! People have argued about "g-o-d" for thousands of years. "Is there a god? What is he like? Is he all-powerful? Does he care about people? How can we please him, or at least not rankle him?" How would you like people to talk about you like that? I know it would bother me a lot. It makes me want to apologize for the times I philosophized about "god" myself.

Our Heavenly Father is real, is big, is more of all things excellent. But He Himself is simple. Really! He showed Himself to me.

Father delights in His Son, Jesus, who perfectly reflects His own holy character and love. The Son of the Father loves rightness and hates twisted wickedness. This is why Father invests all authority, all judgment, all wealth in His glorious Son.

From way back as far as God has been God, Father has been in dialog. Deep things in His heart are shared by Jesus, who understands willingly and enthusiastically. And their Spirit just bubbles with joy over the Father's imagination and glories with respect for the Son who carries out Father's desires. Forever there have been love, respect, honor, joy.

When Father came up with adding mankind to the creatures and angels by creating a sparkling universe, Jesus danced with delight before the Father. The Spirit hovered over all and filled Adam and Eve with life. Jesus used to walk in the Garden to dialog over their questions and new discoveries. Together they were going to expand Paradise to the whole planet. Even now, with Eden turned to cement, Father still likes His children to talk with Him. Our prayers are a pleasure to Him, just like when you climbed up on my lap to ask me things many years ago.

Heaven even has a Council Chamber for His creatures to consult together. The angels make their suggestions. Humans come to listen to God's wisdom and to bring their heart's desire on how Father should run the universe. Amazingly He takes our pleas into consideration, when they reflect His own understanding. Of course He has the last word on the timing and the means of accomplishment. But that is why I used to love to consult with Father, because He always took me seriously!

People find it hard to believe that God likes feedback. He cares about how we feel and what we really want. He said there is a deep connection between our delight in Him and Him giving us the desires of our hearts. We see how feedback is built into the way He works. The human body is a perfect example of how every part is connected to every other, when it is healthy. Feedback even tells the body when one part is sick. This feedback principle is why the U. S. Constitution is so unique, allowing the People and the Government to work together. God wants our feedback on what is going to happen in His universe too.

I wanted to visit the Council Chamber to see it with my new eyes. When I prayed on earth, I knew that Father saw me on one of the upper rows of white marble. My heart always wanted to get to the front rows, where I could hear what others were saying, but I did get closer.

I left the great dome of God's temple and walked the shiny streets, poking into palaces, meeting old/new friends. This time though, Theokaris, a teaching angel, came up behind me. "Welcome, Martin. Let me take you where you desire." (I didn't even need to say anything!) We went in one of the many gateways which, it turned out, led to the Throne Room. "You used to sit over there in that row of seats. " I saw countless rows of marble seats in a semicircle around the throne. There were many aisles so people could walk down front to be heard. There was a vast space around the throne where angels could hover. "Now you can listen in to Father's wisdom as heaven prepares for our King's return to earth. You and your team mates are assembling a mounted army for the final assault.

"Can you see, we are a team? Father, Son and Holy Spirit share and work together. Jesus and Father's family (the Body of Christ) work on Father's commands together with the angelic armies, so Jesus can be king over all the earth. Even a married man and woman are a miniature team, where God brings two people into a new unity that never existed before! The beauty of this kind of synergy was spoiled for us. One member of the heavenly team wanted to take over and not play his part any more. Lucifer wanted to take God's

Son's place. Oh, what horror that was!"

"How did it happen?" I asked. "The mystery of evil has fascinated us humans for generations."

"It was a long time ago, earth time, but the universe has been plagued by destruction ever since. Lucifer was the covering Kerub closest to Jesus and Father's throne. He was magnificent, covered with stones of fire and filling the glory with music. He had a place in the heavenly Council. I don't know why, but one day he slipped. He perverted the good that Father had given him and made it twisted evil. Outwardly he was still wondrous to look at, but his eyes were dark. Darkness had never before existed. Instead of radiating God's light and life, he was sucking up all goodness to keep it for himself. His eyes revealed the "black hole" in his heart that was willing to destroy the Throne, the angels, and God's new creation for his own imperious ambition.

"No wonder then that Father kicked Lucifer out of heaven! But kick him where? God had to set aside outer darkness to match the internal darkness of Lucifer's heart. Somehow Lucifer took a third of the angels with him, when he became Satan, the Opposer. They are a hopeless army, but an angry one. They can only take, because they have nothing good to give.

"Before The War, we were all occupied with worship and creating the new universe. Many angels were assigned as stars. No one needed weapons, as there were no enemies. But one day, Archangel Michael trumpeted assembly. Suddenly the flame of love in me flared up. The flame of God appeared in my hand, looking like a two-edged sword. I reached out my arm and other angels fled into darkness. The bigger angels and Lucifer, the Kerub, bullied smaller spirits into going with them.

"They immediately regretted giving in. Instead of shining with God's glory, their lights went out. It was an eclipse of the angels. Lucifer still has a reflected glory humans sometimes see, but nothing like the brilliance he once had in Father's presence."

Lucifer, now Satan, may not shine with his original glory, but we humans sure have been impressed with what's left! That's because we no longer know God as He really is.

Father amazes me. He is so straightforward. Only pure and holy from the inside out: He can never hide, or lie, or be anything else but God. It's not a limitation of course, but it sure does set Him up for pain. You see, the best that Father can give to anyone is Himself. He Himself is good, is blessing, is joy or love or whatever else His creatures want and need. Not bodily life or health or wealth or friendship or reputation can sustain us, or satisfy us. Humans think these will satisfy them, but they are only temporary substitutes. Only God Himself can satisfy us. Father is the source of all our being.

Being is Father's best invention. He thought of light and sun and oceans and dolphins and grass and pterodactyls and platypuses. And He made men and women and sex and love and children. Then He invited all His new partners to feast on all the fruits He had created for us. But what happened?

Theokaris described Jesus walking in the Garden of Delight that evening, looking for his co-workers, Adam and Eve. What a disappointment he had, when he found them hiding from their best friend.

"The sneaky Red Serpent had fooled Eve into tasting what looked so beautifully appealing, but dragged them away from the Father and into death. Even hardheaded Adam went along with the ploy and chose the knowledge of good and evil. Jesus had warned them not to eat, not to seek power over good and evil. Instead of increasing knowledge and power, they lost their glory like Lucifer had.

"When I saw Adam and Eve just after Jesus brought them together, I clapped my hands over his majestic achievement. They glowed so much with human glory that I didn't even notice they had no clothes on. But now, when they crawled out of the bushes, they looked so, so human, so frail and shrunken, almost. They were naked of their former glory.

"Jesus had to limit the effects of their sin to preserve the human race and the planet. To keep men from spoiling the whole planet at once, Jesus commanded weeds and frustrated work. To keep women from ruling over everyone, he put them under husbands and childbirth. The Red Serpent was no longer allowed to roam freely, but was made to eat dust. Two of the kerubim were detailed to keep all humans from eating fruit off the Tree of Life. That way they could die and stop sinning.

"The most heart wrenching thing Jesus said was that he himself would take back what had just been lost. He said, 'The fruit of a woman's body shall be wounded by the Serpent, but that man will crush the Serpent's head.' Back then I wondered what he meant, but now I know. It would cost Jesus and his Father everything to fulfill that promise to Eve."

I could not tell if Theokaris wanted to cry or laugh. I saw he loved Jesus and he even loved us miserable humans. He obviously cares how we work together to achieve Father's plan. Even angels are curious how Father will pull off the spectacular ending to this tragic story.

Dear Bekka & Joel

Postcards from Heaven

Heaven Imagined and Reported

by Martin Van Horn

When I met Jesus I saw His
magnificence and His humility.

You reached down for us
Your dirtied hand
Formed man and wife

The finger that wrote
Ten flaming words on stone
Wrote in dust the adulteress free

Plant your blooming life
In the dirt of my clay pot

Dear Bekka and Joel,

It took John the Sent One three years living with Jesus 24/7 to figure out that his Lord had showed him that the Father is only good.

Father never forgets His generous intentions. Evil cannot stop Him. That's why I say He is simple. He is simply love and goodness. There is no deception in Him, so He cannot lie and He cannot tempt anyone else to less than the best. Elder brother John came to the conclusion, "Father is light and in Him is no darkness at all." He had lived with Jesus for those years and had spent much time in the Council Chamber as the Lord's new churches were growing and struggling. And I have come to agree with him through my own struggles. I want to let you know, you can trust Father too.

I guess what humans have never figured out is how this pure and holy God can stay so clean while dealing with fouled up, perverted demons and sinning humans. On earth we twist things to our own hurt and blame God for it. We act as though Satan were our friend and God our enemy. But Father never changes, despite our misconceptions.

He loves life and weddings and kids and banquets. He hates death and sickness and the way His universe is out of joint because of sin. Yet He still loves His creatures. Lucifer He cannot save, but He told Prophet Ezekiel to write a lament over Lucifer's fall. Adam and Eve were given the same chance as everyone else. Every sinner who hates his own evil ways and turns his heart to Father will be heard, when he or she cries out for mercy. Father has no joy in the death of a sinner.

Father is not prejudiced. He does not respect one person more than any another. His door is open to any seeker who knocks. But even rich and famous people must admit how poor they are in Father's eyes when they ask for forgiveness. God loves to be generous to people who are not full of themselves. In fact humility in people reminds Him of His beautiful Son. Jesus is submissive and lowly in his heart toward Father. Whatever Father conceives, Jesus delights to perform, and both of them are full of joy.

In creation Jesus spoke and everything came into existence

except people. With Adam, Jesus had to get his hands dirty. God's Spirit got involved giving living, breathing life to the new man. Even Eve had to be built by hand out of Adam's rib. So when it came to rescuing rebellious, perverted, deceived human beings from the awful effects of Satan's totalitarian regime, spoken words could not do the job. Oh, Jesus spoke volumes to his friend Abraham and his deliverer, Moses. But just telling people the truth could not change their hearts. It could set up government and religion, but not everyone recognized who Jesus was through the words he spoke. Jesus had to get dirty once again.

Here again the Father's heart comes through. He loves His Son and knows that everyone else will too, when they see how beautiful he really is. After all, what does Satan have to offer anyway?

Oh, he's attractive, handsome even. I guess some may find him sexy. What does he have to offer? Power, sneakiness, corruption and wealth sound good to a lot of people. But his gifts of fame or pleasure or control don't last. They can't. Everything he promises he had to steal. And he hates us people almost as much as he hates Father and Jesus. You can tell by his eyes. They are cold dark holes of absolute hardheartedness.

Jesus on the other hand is tender, thoughtful, empathetic, compassionate and generous. He likes to share his love and imagination and to encourage friendship with his creatures. Family and government, creativity and commitment all go together in his mind. His eyes are so full of love that they shine, even flame out with passionate caring. The contrast between these two could not be greater. Obviously every sensible creature will choose Jesus over Satan, right?

Hmm, maybe we aren't so sensible!

Father was so confident in His Son that He chose him to go redeem the sons of Adam and daughters of Eve. Jesus had to give up his immortality, his glory, his reputation and power to become a human baby. But He and His Father never gave up their intimate relationship, even though young Jesus in Nazareth had to grow up into maturity. Jesus would have to go down into enemy territory and risk death and disease and injury. He would be despised and rejected by many, even his own family.

Just so people would not be attracted to the Son for the same reasons they followed Satan, Jesus had no sexy good looks. He was an ordinary looking, strong young Jewish carpenter. Some people would see his heart, not just his style.

Surrounded by enemies, rebels against God's law and God's holiness, who raged against His standards, "We want our own ruler, not God's! We want to set our own standards, not be shackled by heaven's commands!" God just laughed. He knew how it would all turn out. He had already designated the King who would rule the world. It was His Son, the human Jesus! For thirty some years it did not look that way, but God knew.

His perfect King needs no power; He willingly gave it all up. King Jesus takes no offense at His enemies; He forgives them. He does not rule by appearances; He rules by rightness, whatever people may think. He claims nothing for himself; He gave it all up, tortured, bleeding profusely and executed by crucifixion. But the Father could not leave His Son in the grave. After three days, He raised him up to new life and eternal power and glory such as you can see today.

Father knew He could commit everything to Jesus. Jesus created and taught His representatives on earth, man and woman. Jesus became one of them to redeem them back again. Now Jesus will build His Church out of people who recognize who He is and with them come back to earth to rule until the end of the age.

In the meantime, Jesus' representatives on earth speak His words to people who don't know him yet. His words are spirit and they are life, so God's Spirit uses them to make people into new creatures. We are stuck in the old body on earth until we graduate up here to our Home, but the Spirit gives us a taste of full life even there on earth.

Precious in Father's sight is the death of His saints. Because they spread Father's love on earth, they are sorely missed when they leave. But the saints on earth know what awaits them when they die, so they have joy in anticipation. And when Father's kids are carried Home, they each get a parade like I did. Pain, persecution, rejection, fear are all forgotten. But there are no shortcuts on our earthly journeys. Father works with His children to bring good into all things, so we become mature like

Jesus through our sufferings. If we try to cut the process short, we can't understand Father when we get here either. Earth is the time His kids have to get to know their Father's heart of love, so they can hear what He has to say when they get Home.

Dear Bekka & Joel

Postcards from Heaven
_____
Heaven Imagined and Reported

by Martin Van Horn

What a place! No drugstores, no funeral homes, no hospitals!

Eternal youth!
The search is over!

No fountain, no cream, no doctor
Cleansed by the blood
Created by God's Spirit new

The body has caught up to it's spirit
Forever alive

Dear Bekka and Joel,

The Real Church is assembling up here and I'm excited to be in the midst of her. We are getting ready to bring the Kingdom of Heaven down to earth. I can only tell you of a few preparations, but it is really big. When I look around, I can see why that will be such a change for the better.

I thought you would be fascinated with some things that have jumped out at me. You know how sometimes you're in a new location and everybody there thinks the way they live is completely normal. Only you haven't quite become accustomed to their way of life, so you get a peculiar feeling and wonder, "What's different here?" That's what happened to me.

You know the feeling, "I just feel like something is missing?" Well I never have that feeling any more. Since arriving, my experience has been so right and satisfying. That made it all the more startling to realize what I'm missing. There are no signs of death!

You never see cripples, wheelchairs, crutches, bent age, or shrivelled limbs. The streets are lined with glowing Homes being built of gold, silver and brilliant jewel stones (not little, finger ring sizes either). Suddenly the missing slums, hospitals, taverns, mortuaries, churches, funeral parlors, gambling halls, porn clubs, video rentals, insurance agencies, and drugstores have all jumped out at me. No need! No desire! We never miss them!

People are wonders. Each person is dignified. Old people have wisdom and child-like wonder about them, but they are not weak or frail or dried up. They are vital and smooth with dynamic energy. Young people are relaxed and secure and full of expectation, as though they can't wait for what the Lord has coming. Children are always together, playing, dancing, studying, worshipping. Theirs is a serious play, not foolish, because they know there is so much ahead for them. Many of them are the martyrs, murdered before birth, who have to do their growing here, because it was denied them on earth. They pray for other children on earth to be granted the destinies God had planned for them, but their parents had cut off.

Most of the "time" we gather together before the Throne.

But in between, we stroll and talk and visit at Home or in the gardens. Exciting as a novel or movie are the stories the saints tell of the intriguing paths they have journeyed to arrive at Home. Some met the Lord in a dream or in a preacher. Others cried out to the God they did not know, because they were in pain or need. Sometimes you see a person you met just once on earth and you shared with them what you had and to whom you gave no more thought; but now you hear, that was the breakthrough of glory into their lives.

Personally I love to hear tales of the Sent Ones, missionaries who deliberately took upon themselves hardships because that is what their Lord had done. Some travelled and some stayed home. One of the Twelve, named Thomas, walked all the way from Israel to India. Jim flew to the jungle to translate the Bible and was speared to death. Some loved strangers and others loved their prison wardens enough to bring them Home. Richard was tortured by Communists, but Jesus was with him in prison. All tell the same song of pain and joy: their Lord was there. He led, He suffered, He conquered, and He comforted them. Now they have so many friends here, who were able to join them on the journey Home just because they gave out love when they received hate.

I mentioned the gardens. Another thing you don't see are large farms dominating the landscape. Everyone gets their own garden to tend. This is Father's Paradise, with room for all, work and fruitfulness, plenty to have and to share. No weeds, no drought, no bugs, just pleasing trees short and tall, flowers pink or orange, vines and shrubs live here. It reminds me of sunny days, vine-draped- fences and the aromas of wild roses or honeysuckle.

Spacious, that's Home. I don't know if I'll ever see all of it. But yet it is not too big. On earth walking and travelling were something to plan for. How long? What to take? How costly? Here at Home, travel is never tiring. I can walk or I arrive instantly, or I fly. It all depends. I'm not sure what it depends on, just like I'm not sure why I can communicate with any being I meet, but that's the way it is.

Maybe one of the reasons travel is no barrier, is because time is so unimportant and so is gravity. The only thing heavy here is the Glory of God. When you get close to Him from whom all life flows, you can feel His overwhelming Presence coming over you like a pressure. It's like trying to swim upstream against a river. Everything else is so light in comparison. I can go over or up or down, wherever I need to go. I can go immediately, or I can take time to go slowly, whatever is right. It's wonderful! Whee!

That must be why I'm just now noting the absence of automobiles, buses, gas stations, trucks, bulldozers, bikes and skates. I'm sure you think I'm "out of it," not to have noticed their absence first off, since on earth they are hard to avoid. And I guess that's true; I'm out of it down there because I'm "with it" up here. The truth of real values has overwhelmed the details that used to preoccupy me. Jesus and the Father are not only over there somewhere for me to visit, but they are in my heart and mind; they're in my conversation and singing; they're in my thinking and questioning. They are life, and the details only start to come to mind later.

I'm sure you can't digest all these startling descriptions about what is here at Home so every-day wonderful. But you already know that sin and death have to come to an end. Jesus came not only to save sinning humans, but also to destroy all the works of the Devil. The Enemy is behind death, sickness, debilitation, insecurity, abuse, war, poverty, and cold-heartedness. There is no more Enemy, only the Father, our Friend and Lover, our Source and joy forever. We have nothing to fear, because things only get better, never worse. Even Jesus is looking forward to inheriting His unadulterated Kingdom. The Father shall be all in all and Jesus will reign over a perfect People, who rejoice to work together doing whatever He says. I'm sure the Father has some new eternal project in mind for us. That's all He ever thinks about: how Jesus' wonderful character can be displayed over and over, everywhere in newer and newer ways.

I'm glad I gave up my clinging to things on earth that only seemed so important. They have all been left behind. This is for you, to help you consider what real life is. Is it what you see; what you desire? Or is life the eternal things you can pull down to earth right now: love, forgiveness, patience, joy, gentleness and so on. Look beyond what your eyes can see. Think of who

Jesus is and what He has done so you can enjoy what He enjoys.

As our elder brother Paul said, "Set your mind on things above." You begin to think about things that last forever. Time is not so much the factor, as is the "long-lastingness." If you ask me how long I've been here, I couldn't say. I don't know how eternal life relates to your time on earth. Maybe it matters, but I'm sure we'll find out when it does. I know the glorious people up here will go back to restore the Beautiful Planet, but I don't know when. I see horses gathering. I hear trumpets blowing. I hear angels trooping. A blazing army with no guns, no artillery, no tanks, no planes, no bombs, just sheer power is assembling. Earth will be overwhelmed with fear and thankfulness.

Dear Bekka & Joel

Postcards from Heaven

Heaven Imagined and Reported

by Martin Van Horn

Heaven is extremely relaxed, nothing to hide. Everyone understands, we all enjoy each other.

Come, join me
I do not want to walk alone anymore

Here we are
Let us walk together
From birth till the End
But there is no end

Dear Bekka and Joel,

You remember Sharon spending so much time and effort counselling problems, saving marriages, bringing Jesus into hurting hearts. That was a premonition of reality.

Not just things are missing; human relationship problems are gone too! This is one you'll like: people don't argue or fight. I've been here long enough and seen enough conversations to know what I'm talking about. And it's not that people are just being "nice." Like I said, everyone is relaxed and honest, because the Lord is everywhere and He has revealed everything. We are all open to each other.

On earth we kept secrets. The bad parts were hidden, we hoped. (Observant people like you could see our body language, our outbursts, our lives and could tell something was rotten underneath.) And the worst secrets were the ones we tried to hide from ourselves. We lied to ourselves all the time.

"I'm doing this for your own good," I might say, when really it was not just your good in mind, but also justification for my own selfishness. How often we used to claim great excuses for awful behaviour? "You made me angry." "I would have been so patient, if you hadn't been so annoying." "I wanted to pray, but I didn't have time." "I love you, but I'm busy."

Everyone else was at fault, because their problems were so plainly visible. Logically, you would think such obvious poisons would make me avoid the same in myself, but no; in reaction to your problems, I justify myself doing the same things to others. Only in myself, these poisons now became elegant means to great ends. "Let me explain why you are wrong, so I can set you straight." "Other people may be mean and impatient, but I am goal-oriented and forthright."

Here at Home, we can't lie to ourselves any more. I am who I am, no more and no less. I am a saint, loved by the Supreme Father, cleansed by the Perfect Son, full of the Holy Spirit of God. His light has revealed and removed all darkness. It has been forgiven and cleansed by the blood of Jesus' sacrifice, precious in his Father's eyes and now in mine also. Praise to the Lord of glory, who has raised me to enjoy His glory and shine with it forever!

Not only have I received Father's forgiveness, but so have all the others here. Once forgiving my tormentors seemed so unjust, so frustrating. Not until I saw my need of God's forgiveness, did I see the significance of sin and holding offences against other people. If sin led to death and I sinned, I deserved death, death forever. That God had sent His perfect Son to take onto Himself my sin, my pain, my condemnation and my death, all in order to forgive me, was the revelation of who I was and who He is. Only after receiving God's forgiveness, letting me go without punishment, did I begin to see why I had to forgive people. Forgiveness frees up God's love to flow, God's gift of healing to release resentment, God's desire for faithfulness to restore broken relationships. Father gets excited when we agree with Him and up here we all enjoy the fruits of His forgiveness. That's why we would rather enjoy relationships than break them.

Even honest people have different points of view, naturally. Back on earth this often led to nasty disagreements, because different priorities and differing interpretations of facts turned human frailties into life-or-death conflicts. Up here we share in God's point of view. We know all things are relative, relative to Him who is the truth and never changes. He has made us so diverse and fascinating, that we would rather find out how our partner reflects the infinite wisdom of God, than try to be right. God is always true, even if all of us have missed some part of the truth. So from now on, we can all help each other find out the parts of the truth we have not yet experienced. Learning and growing are not lonely, bookish occupations any more. We make them into a party. "Hey, come on over to my place and let's share, so we can learn more about our Lord and His ways. Can we get together now? Shall we invite some other saints to join us?"

So when we come together, only one Person is in charge, teaching us all. And He has defeated and removed the Enemy from our minds. Before, the black Liar made things seem so, that simply weren't so. He made it seem like we were all alone in that world, with no one to care or understand. Each of us was so desperate to live and prosper, that we would use other people and even attack them if we did not get what we wanted.

God was so distant, so out of touch with our needs down on earth that we thought He was the enemy, responsible for our woes. How many millions sided with the Devil, hurting themselves and each other, meanwhile blaming their woes on God? We thought God should take our side in the struggle of life, come down, yield to our demands, and make "Big Me" into a king.

Interestingly, now that the Betrayer, who wanted to be god instead of the Lord, is no longer pulling us into his lies; the Father can indeed make His Children into the kings and queens He had originally intended us to be. King Adam and Queen Eve were to rule Earth, making it into a paradise like Eden, working together with the Lord, their mentor. You know too well that Father's plan has been delayed by a few thousand years. But now is the time for us humans to begin again. Once I laid down my life and my own will, my ambitions and intentions, taking up the life Jesus invented just for me, I then could begin to exercise authority in the Lord's name.

It began on earth. People call it prayer. Really it is human kings consulting with the Counsels of Heaven. I used to come before the Throne of Grace with my requests and my questions. The Father listened to me and I wanted to hear Him. Eventually I wanted to know what was on His heart, what would glorify Jesus and satisfy His desire to bless His People. Then I knew my prayers were heard. From this viewpoint, we can see these prayers come up to the Father. It is not far from the heart of the saint to the heart of the Father. Pure, undefiled requests come before the Throne as a golden cloud, the pleasant odour of perfumed incense. They bring joy to the Father.

Interestingly, since the distance is not far to earth either, sometimes the Lord's presence appears to the praying saints as well. They too sense, or even see, the golden cloud of God's glory on earth. So as their prayers ascend as golden smoke in heaven, the Presence of the Glorious One is felt back on earth as well. Praise the Lord!

The Father is storing up the prayers of billions of saints from centuries of yearning, "Come Kingdom of Heaven! Your will be done here on earth as it is in Heaven!" The answer will arrive soon!

The remaking of earth is in training up here for now. Soon it will take place down on the planet you live on. Father revealed to John a lot of the things that have to happen first, like the meteor bombardment of the year 2029 that scientists have already predicted and its attendant wreckage. World politics are setting the stage as well, lining up against God's Land and God's People.

Dear Bekka & Joel

Postcards from Heaven

Heaven Imagined and Reported

by Martin Van Horn

Billions have prayed for it and here comes God!

Knock, knock
"May I come in?"

Meeting with Moses
On a golden box
Dancing with King David
In an open tent
Filling Solomon's sanctuary
With floods of glory
Teaching disciples
On the mountainside

You want to live where we live
we say, "Come, Lord."

Dear Bekka and Joel,

You have thousands of years of history to look back on for you to see God's plan for mankind and for your destiny.

First there was Paradise. It was a Garden of Pleasure, watered by four rivers, touched by heavenly dew, and filled with all plants and all animals. Our First Father and Mother were crafted there by the hand and breath of our Maker. They walked and talked with animals, each other, and the Maker Himself. Home was just around the corner from Paradise.

But First Father and Mother were cut off from the life of blessed work and joy. For some weird reason they sided with the Enemy and lied about the Creator's goodness and generosity. They thought they could take over for the Wonderful One, but of course they could not. Father's orchard grew such luminous fruits, that they almost seemed magical. Maybe I would have thought like they did: fruits were not only beautiful but potent as well. They chose the wrong forbidden fruit.

They must have thought their glorious glow belonged to themselves, and they could do with it whatever they wanted. Trying to become the Maker themselves turned out to be impossible. Their light went out. They lost their glorious glow. Everything became a chore—working, talking, traveling, bearing children, everything. The only divine leftover was the guard at the door. The Lord stationed 15-foot tall Kerubim at the gate to keep people out, so they could not grab eternal fruit and live forever in darkness and dying.

The Maker never forgot his children. People saw the Messengers He sent once in a while, often while sleeping. These angels warned them of danger, of slipping and falling, of going too far until they ended up down in Death. Way back when Job lived, He helped them in their needs. And some children called on Him for help. He especially loves it when we call out for mercy, because He delights in us. It brings out the best in Him.

One of His friends got here early. He must have called out and received that Father mercy. Enoch was a shepherd, but he walked with God as he herded sheep. Every day they shared about everything, until one day, Enoch looked back and earth was gone. He had wandered from grassland into Heaven and the Lord simply kept him here. Unfortunately, Enoch was an exception.

Of all the beautiful places on the "blue planet," there is one that's special; it's an outpost of Heaven on earth. It's called Mount Zion. Once the King of Heaven met his friend there. Melchizedek (King of righteousness) ruled in Salem (Peace) on this holy hill. He met Abram there after a military victory. Abram brought a tenth of the booty from defeating his enemies and gave it to Melchizedek. The King blessed his friend with God's blessing.

Zion will one day be the landing pad for the King's return. But in the meantime it has been God's holy dwelling and the place of greatest sacrilege. Let me outline this drama.

God renamed Abram to be Abraham, "Father of Multitudes." His descendants increased over the years. They left the Mount Zion area for Egypt. For 430 years, a little spot in Egypt had God's hand upon it. In the midst of rejection, misunderstanding, and slavery, the Israelites enjoyed the blessings and protection of heaven in the land of Goshen, at the mouth of the Nile River. When the Lord judged the gods of the Egyptians by the 10 plagues, the land of Goshen was unharmed. God loved to live with His people.

Moses was the deliverer God sent to bring the Israelite nation out of slavery in Egypt and into a godly civilization in His Promised Land. To be godly they needed to have God in their midst. God took their leader to heaven so He could show how to represent His Home by earthly architecture. Moses saw the Throne, the 7 spirits of God, the incense of prayers, and the covering Beings. These he represented in the desert outside Israel in a tent. The Lord throned upon the Mercy Seat of the Ark under the wings of two Kerubim.

Outside the veil, an altar of incense represented heavenly prayers. The 7-armed menorah represented the seven spirits of God. When the workmen finished following Moses' instructions, the glory of God came down and took over. God camped for a while in the middle of 12 tribes, living in the Tabernacle showing them how to worship a holy God.

King David was the next guest in heaven. Instead of a tent he wanted to build a permanent house for his beloved Lord

God. Prophet Nathan told him God would build David a house, a lineage, but that he was not the man to build the Lord a building. David gave to his son, Solomon, the heavenly plan how to build the Temple out of stone, wood, and gold. Again God's throne was represented by the golden mercy seat under the kerubim in the Holy of Holies.

Can you believe it, God actually lived in that tent and in that stone Temple? To think the Lord of the Universe, Creator of all things wanted so much to live among His people, that He shrank His glorious presence down to such a small space! What He won't do to show He loves the people He has chosen!

The next two men to visit the Throne came during the decline of God's people. The prophet Isaiah saw the Lord, high and lifted up. The Lord gave him a message of warning and comfort to a people tempted to stray away to other gods. Since Isaiah did not succeed in halting the decline, God showed Himself to Ezekiel, revealing His chariot throne searching the earth for a place to rest. He decided to leave His beloved Temple building, because the priests had brought in occult spirits He found abominable. Ezekiel also received revelation of a new temple, where the King would someday come.

God's people corrupted themselves and then they corrupted the Temple. Solomon's empty temple was leveled by enemies. It was rebuilt by King Herod, but remained empty, until one day. God shrinking His glory to fit into a tent or temple was not enough. He shrank His glory into a baby's body. Beyond incredible, huh?

In Bethlehem, the Lord used to meet in the shepherd's field with the young man, David. That's the same field where the angels came to announce the birth of the Son of God to the local shepherds. The angel armies of heaven sang their joy at heaven invading earth. Mary of Nazareth gave birth to Jesus that night. She must have been overwhelmed, knowing that the Most High had conceived in her. And that boy grew up, visiting the empty temple when he was newborn and again at age twelve. Then at thirty, after the Spirit of God had come upon him with power, he again visited the empty temple, saying he would rebuild it in three days. What a scandal he caused! But he did it.

The Temple of the Living God was now a human body. Very

few saw it. Once on a mountaintop, Peter, James, and John saw Jesus blaze as bright as the sun. He was talking with Moses and Elijah about His Homegoing, because Jesus considered His death to be His glorifying. Outside Jerusalem on the Cross, in His blood and fatal weakness, there He showed the Devil and the world that God is love. There purity triumphed over injustice and wickedness. There God condemned all sin in the body of His Son and did away with it forever. Glory to God! No compromises allowed! No compromises taken.

The Father was pleased with His Son and gave Him back the glory that He had had in Heaven before becoming an infant on earth. Today He is the Lord of Glory with nail marks in His hands and a spear wound in His side. We can see Him in His true identity.

I see Him every day. He has transformed me by His penetrating love. I want everything He wants and nothing that He does not want. Back on Earth, He is building a new Temple, not made with hands, not constructed of stone and wood. It is you and you and a billion other believers inhabited by the Holy Spirit of God. We are the Real Church, the invisible divine Temple! No one can destroy it and soon it will no longer be invisible.

We're coming back to earth soon! We have a lot of good things to bring with us!

Dear Bekka & Joel

Postcards from Heaven

Heaven Imagined and Reported

by Martin Van Horn

What should I wear to a glory party?
Let the King pick out my wardrobe.

Utopia
Camelot
Knight in shining armour

What about a peasant
Killed on a Cross?
And if God made Him King
Over all the Earth
Inviting all peasants
To share His Throne
Would you come?

Dear Bekka and Joel,

    Purity and dedication on the inside show on the outside. Here we glow with the power of life and our white robes blaze with the good work the Father prepared for us. Across the chest we wear the gold sash of rightness and around the waist we wear the gold belt of truth.

    Instead of colours, cut, cloth, leather, jewellery, or hairdos, each person reveals who they are by a rainbow twinkle. Clothes reveal who we are instead of concealing who we are.

    If you wear what others are wearing, does that make you part of the crowd? If you wear something different from everybody else, do you have to manufacture your own apparel? Do your clothes prove you are rich, or sophisticated, or well-educated, or well-indoctrinated by advertising? So whom do people see when they look at you? Are you attractive, or blah, or off-putting? It's no wonder people on earth think more about what they wear, than who they are. "How do I feel today?" "Whom do I have to impress tonight?"

    Here at Home there is something real, a solid security in being happy with who Jesus has made me to be. My glow will never fade with age. People recognize my stature in God without ever quibbling, or belittling. No one compares my blazing righteousness with their own or anyone else's, because it is a feeble offshoot of the Original Glory blasting us every moment from the Only One who is always Himself Glory.

    It is such a privilege to be part of the Lord's party that fashion never comes to mind. My imagination just shades the twinkle of my clothes every time I rejoice in a new idea. How I feel is never in doubt. I always feel great and my clothes show it. When I look at other people or other Creatures, I see how they embody the Great Imagination, the Unstoppable Creator. It's not seasonal fashion, it's continuous sparkling, blazing verve. Everybody gets to be creatively personal, reflecting the Great Person who made us each so special.

    Once upon a time, people loved to shop. Here we don't shop. We create, we receive gifts. We revel in having and in receiving and in giving. I have all I can want. So does everyone else. And then the Father gives us more. Happiness is dead; long live joy!

These last postcards have been about things we are probably all glad to get rid of or at least trade in on something better. But another change is far more profound and radical.

You can read it yourself in the Revelation given to St. John, "There is no night there." Have you ever thought about that?

It means there are no more cycles, no repetitions of daily, seasonal, annual, or whenever changes. Some things are too good to change. And here at Home we have gotten acquainted with things that always have been, with no need to change. They just are and are and will be.

"No night" means no loss of brightness, no loss of awareness, no unknown, no hiding, no aloneness. Back in your world, the old earth, sunshine and star shine dissipated in the universal darkness of space, sustained by a supply of exploding hydrogen. Here glory simply is and never stops because it streams endlessly from the divine fountain.

Think back to the Beginning. God said, "Let there be light." Well, what an explosion that was! Yet, before there was light there was Glory!

How can I describe something which earth does not have any more? How can I describe something more substantial than all reality humans can sense? There is nothing to compare to it and no words in human experience to make it manageable. Try "Solid" "Streaming" "Visible and tangible" "Bright" "Overwhelming" "Addictive" "Consuming fire."

We have no adequate vocabulary, yet we humans are attracted to God like moths are attracted to a candle flame. That unknown, unseen holy glory pulls us. If we get too close, we burn up (in our earthly bodies, anyway). Yet we cannot stand to be too far away either. We want that fire.

Now that Fire has me. I have a new, spirit body that can stand the blaze. My body blazes with shared glory. The blazing eyes of love have burned up all that is inferior and rejected by the Holy One. So I love Him too. And He has projects for me to do. It turns out I am on one of the teams bringing glory to the mess people have made of the earth.

God kind of snuck up on me to get me involved with them. Let me tell you how I met the great revival preacher, Jonathan Edwards.

Dear Bekka & Joel

Postcards from Heaven

Heaven Imagined and Reported

by Martin Van Horn

I got to look down at the people and places I left when I died. The struggle goes on.

You have to suffer
Be born
Die
Live

Your body says, Yes
Your spirit says, No
God says, Up
The Devil says, Down

You have to choose wisely

Dear Joel and Bekka,

As I was passing by the Temple in Heaven, I turned to my neighbor, an amazingly wise looking gentleman. He said, "I've been praying for you in New England for around 300 years, since I preached in Northampton, Massachusetts. There have been many ups and downs in the spiritual receptivity there. The enemy has flooded in idolatry and perversion through the intellectual pride so dominant there, especially where the Holy Spirit once brought such light and salvation. But the Lord who builds His Church keeps sending in new workers to accomplish His divine ends."

My eyes widened as I recognized that great revival preacher and theologian, Jonathan Edwards, "I read your book on godly affections. That's how I found out growth in holiness is the only indicator of a true work of the Spirit. And your sermon on heaven, where you assert that heaven gets better and better, really inspired me."

He explained, "Oh, yes, heaven and hell were two of my most frequent topics, when I preached. People need to know that earth is not where their real life is experienced. Spiritual reality gives them a right view of work and wealth or pain and disappointment. The Father wants His children to look at life the way He does."

I protested, "But don't you wish you could go back and set people straight. After looking at the struggle between sin and salvation or demons and angels from here, I feel like the people I knew on earth need me more than ever. This isn't just some 'reality TV' show; it's a real gladiator fight between the forces of good and evil."

Edwards replied, "I understand what you are thinking. I too have regarded the desperate situation as being in need of my newly enlightened ministry. However, we cannot go back. We pray along with the saints below. As you have seen, prayers of the Little Ones achieve much up here. I have heard many encouraging reports from new arrivals that Lord Jesus is changing the atmosphere in many locales. Seekers sense His Presence and receive healings, revelations and other gifts. The Bridegroom is showering His Bride with love.

"I believe the Gathering Angels will bring hundreds of millions of needy persons into the Family of Father God very quickly, even though the enemy is spreading violence and fear.

"You must come with me to the training palace. Have you received your assignment for the Return?"

I looked at him questioningly, "The Return?"

"You understand. The Lord will return to earth with His holy ones and we shall judge the peoples of the earth. The first things we will give attention to are the removal of the destruction wrought by the asteroid strike of 2029 foretold in elder brother John's Revelation. Dwellers of earth will need much comfort and teaching in God's ways to understand what has happened. The removal of hundreds of millions of believers will leave them baffled. I have been assigned to soil cleaning and re-seeding the earth. Let us go and see what assignment is written for you."

My, O my, this was a shock. Back to school again. Looks like we never stop learning. The heavenly city will be coming down to earth soon (comparatively soon at least). We can see it up here in heaven, sparkling like a diamond, except the jewel is hundreds of miles square and hundreds of miles high. Her three levels are suspended one above the other. Eventually it will cover all the holy lands that belong to God's nation of Israel. The brilliance of the Son of God will be all the illumination she ever needs. Then all creation will witness the beauty of the Son's Bride, as billions of redeemed saints shine with the glory of their Bridegroom. For now we are all scattered over space and time, but at that point we will all be together and what our Lord has accomplished in our lives and bodies will light up the universe.

My deeds of obedience have supplied Jesus, the master builder, with the materials for my mansion up there. I am excited to see its walls and columns and flowers and vines. It will feel just like me, just like home, custom-made. Somewhere in that shining city is my very own dwelling place. You'll have to come over for lunch when we get there.

Jonathan was leading me to a great building with many doors and large windows. We approached a door leading to a library, with floor to ceiling books. A recording angel looked at me and reached down a thick book, opening to my name. "I see you have always enjoyed living on the sea coast. You will be learning how to turn poisoned waters into the sweet water of life. Many will die of bitter waters and only sweet, fresh water can restore the earth so you can reign over a fresh environment. Classes are being held around back by the lagoon."

Now here was an aspect of God's plan I had never thought about. All of creation has been groaning to Father ever since Adam sinned and brought a curse on the ground. All Nature is awaiting the revealing of us sons and daughters of God, so we can set it free to luxuriate as our Creator originally intended. We'll find out what God had in mind and Adam and Eve missed out on. But first I have to learn more about the clean-up process after God's judgments on unrepentant sinners.

Some day there will be a new heavens and a new earth, but first we have to restore this one. It's amazing how Father never wastes anything. My experience back on earth will be part of my preparation for things no mind has yet imagined. Water and rocks and plants and animal, etc., etc. will be free from the perversion of poison or sickness or destruction. Everything we see will reflect the wisdom and glory of our creator. As has been said, even a grain of sand can reveal a world of wonder.

I feel like my postcards are drawing to a close. Classes are starting for me. You can see that by hanging in there, Jesus will bring you through to join us. Tell people it will be worth it all, when we see Him face to face.

Afterword

Around the world, thousands of people have had visions, dreams and visitations from heaven. I have as yet not had any such experience. Nevertheless, God has revealed so much in His Word, the Bible that we should all realize heaven is no figment of human imagination, but rather a fact, a fact so eternally real that the earth pales in comparison. This contrast is felt within the human heart, as King Solomon once wrote, "God has put eternity into man's heart, that men will keep seeking God, not understanding His Creation plan." So each of us hungers for a world we have not seen, but we know must exist. As C. S. Lewis said, "If I find in myself a desire which no experience in this world can satisfy, the most probable explanation is that I was made for another world." I agree.

I congratulate you for reading to the end of my book. Let me add my urging to Peter's letter. Begin a life of faith by realizing your need to be reconciled to the Lord of Glory, because this is the only way to make yourself at home in His heaven. He lives there; it is His Home; everything suits Him and reflects His character. We human beings do not reflect His character and glory. Many cannot enter the Eternal Kingdom: "the fearful, and unbelieving, and the abominable in God's eyes, and murderers, and sorcerers, and idolaters, and all liars, shall have their part in the lake burning with fire and sulphur, which is the unending second death."

Many people delude themselves into thinking they will "go to heaven," because they are "good people." Jesus does not agree. He once said, "Why do you call me 'good?' there is none good but God." So you see, this label "good" does not fit us. Instead, we need to accept God's good news that, although "all have sinned and come short of the glory of God," God laid on the Lord Jesus all our human twistedness and failures. "God made Him, who had never experienced sin, to become our sin; so that in Christ's successful work, we might receive His absolutely undefiled rightness."

If you have knowingly made this exchange: acknowledging your sinful twistedness and failures, seeing it on the Lord Jesus as He died on the Cross; then receiving in place of your sin the rightness of the Lord Himself, who completely pleased God; in that case you have embarked on the splendid journey to the Eternal Glory I have described. "Once you were darkness, but now you are light in the Lord; walk as a child of light."

Congratulations! Together we will worship our magnificent Friend, the Lord of Glory, singing in chorus, "Holy! Holy! Holy!"

About the Author

The Bible says the Kingdom of Heaven belongs to God's "little ones." I remain wide-eyed at the God who does wonders and I want to be like a helium balloon with my imagination in the clouds, but with brain tied to the truths learned at Trinity Evangelical Divinity School.

My talented wife, son and daughter challenge me to open myself to all the ways humans communicate. Hopefully I can open you up to some of the ways God has communicated with us humans as well.

www.ingramcontent.com/pod-product-compliance
Lightning Source LLC
Chambersburg PA
CBHW051711040426
42446CB00008B/834